COLORS
ARE NICE

By ADELAIDE HOLL

Pictures by LEONARD SHORTALL

gb **GOLDEN PRESS**
Western Publishing Company, Inc.
Racine, Wisconsin

Ninth Printing, 1977

Green is nice for trees, I think.
And I like clover blossoms pink.

I like pussy willows gray—
They're really very nice that way.

Red is pretty for a cherry,
Purple for an elderberry,

Yellow for a buttercup.
But I LOVE colors all mixed up!

I like stripes on zebras,

Flowers on rugs,

Polka-dots on ladybugs,
Marble full of wiggly streaks,

Speckled stones you find in creeks,

Insides of shells, all wavy-pearly,
The way the sky looks very early.

I like splashed-together shades in flowers,
Shiny puddles when it showers,

Caterpillars, ringed and wrinkly,
Rainbows on a day that's sprinkly.

I love butterflies and things
With lovely splotchy-colored wings;

Brownish fawns all whitely speckled,
People's faces nicely freckled,

Bright, bright trees in autumn weather,
The sparkles in a peacock feather,

A striped cat,

A spotted pup,

I just LOVE colors all mixed up!

Red, of course, is fine for roses,
And moles look nice with pinkish noses.

White is nice for clouds and snow;
Black for feathers on a crow.

I like the way the sky is blue,
And I like orange oranges, too.

But I LOVE mixed-up colors best—
A baby robin's speckled breast,

Blackish dots on greenish frogs,
Rainbow beetles under logs,

And stripes around a candy cane.

I'm GLAD that colors aren't all plain!